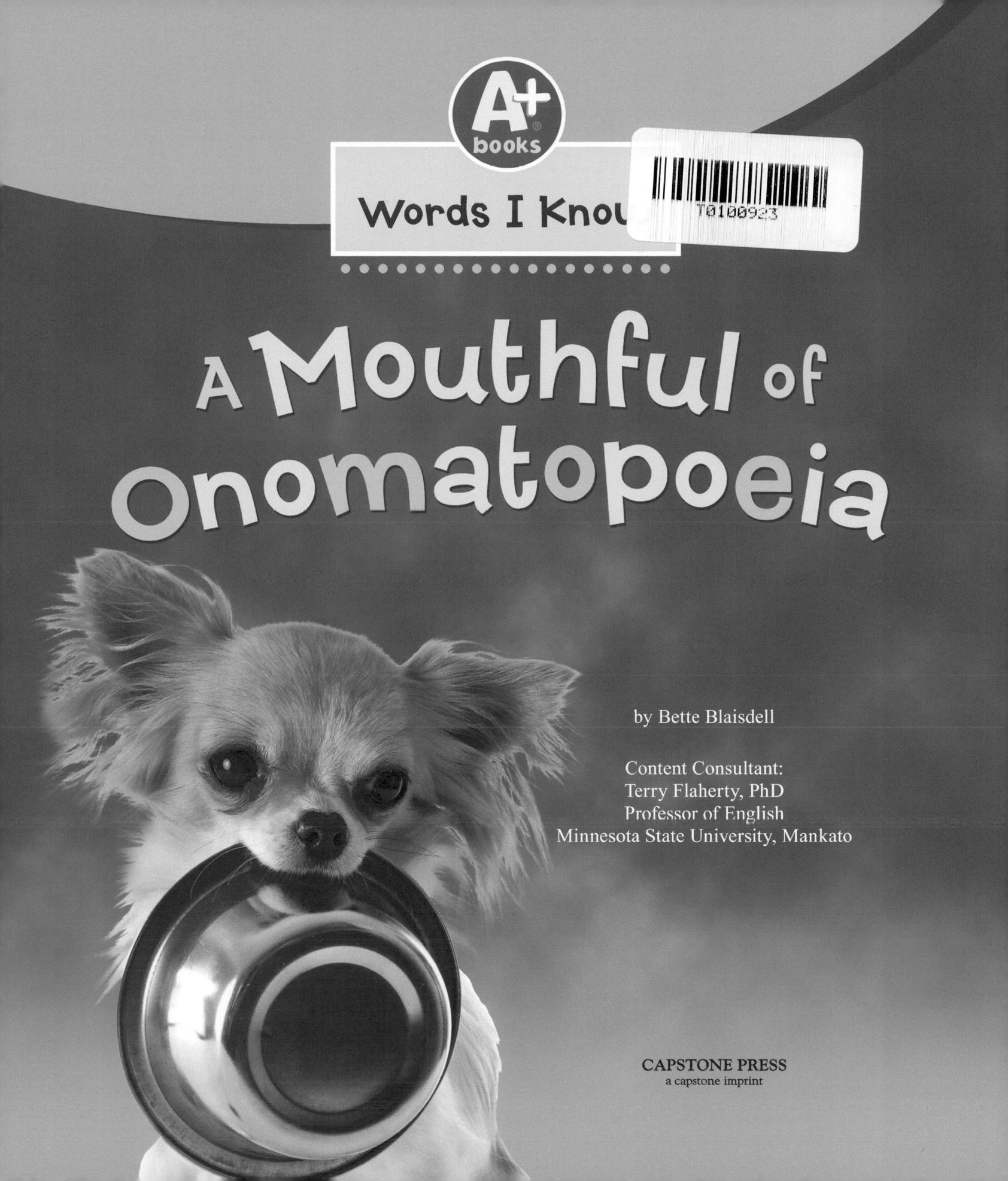

A+ books

Words I Know

T0100923

A Mouthful of Onomatopoeia

by Bette Blaisdell

Content Consultant:
Terry Flaherty, PhD
Professor of English
Minnesota State University, Mankato

CAPSTONE PRESS
a capstone imprint

A+ Books are published by Capstone Press,
1710 Roe Crest Drive, North Mankato, Minnesota 56003
www.capstonepub.com

Copyright © 2014 by Capstone Press, a Capstone imprint. All rights reserved. No part of this publication may be reproduced in whole or in part, or stored in a retrieval system, or transmitted in any form or by any means, electronic, mechanical, photocopying, recording, or otherwise, without written permission of the publisher.

Library of Congress Cataloging-in-Publication Data
Blaisdell, Bette.
A mouthful of onomatopoeia / by Bette Blaisdell.
pages cm.—(A+ books. Words i know.)
Summary: "Full-color photographs and rhyming text introduce and define onomatopoeia"—Provided by publisher.
ISBN 978-1-4765-3939-3 (library binding)
ISBN 978-1-4765-5099-2 (paperback)
ISBN 978-1-4765-5944-5 (eBook PDF)
1. Onomatopoeia—Juvenile literature. I. Title.
P119.B53 2014
428.1—dc23 2013035689

Editorial Credits
Jill Kalz, editor; Juliette Peters, designer; Svetlana Zhurkin, media researcher; Kathy McColley, production specialist

Photo Credits
Shutterstock: 3445128471, 5 (left), AKaiser, 2–3, 4–5 (back), 32, Alan Bailey, 8 (top), Alexander Cherednichenko, 28 (bottom), altanaka, 8 (bottom), Butterfly Hunter, 20 (middle), cynoclub, 1, Darja Vorontsova, 19, Dmitry Morgan, 17 (left), effe45, 23, Eric Isselee, 5 (right), Erni, 10 (bottom), Ferenc Szelepcsenyi, 18, GGrigorov, 29, haak78, 11, IbajaUsap, 20 (bottom), Illya Vinogradov, 7 (top), InnervisionArt, 10 (top), Irina Tischenko, 28 (top), Jaimie Duplass, 22 (bottom), Jean Schweitzer, 12 (top), Karen H. Ilagan, 16 (left), Karin Hildebrand Lau, 30 (bottom), kojihirano, 15 (bottom), Marcel Jancovic, 25 (bottom), Michel Borges, 26, mlorenz, cover, Monkey Business Images, 31, Nanette Grebe, 17 (right), Natursports, 25 (top), Nomad_Soul, 4 (bottom), oliveromg, 30 (top), PhotoStock10, 24, R. Gino Santa Maria, 14 (left), Rob Hainer, 9, Samuel Borges Photography, 14 (right), Sandra Caldwell, 15 (top), spotmatik, 12 (bottom), Stephanie Frey, 22 (top), svic, 20–21 (back), TessarTheTegu, 21 (front), Thomas M. Perkins, 13, Tom Bird, 7 (bottom), Veda J. Gonzalez, 16 (right), Villion van Niekerk, 6 (top), Volodymyr Burdiak, 6 (bottom), ZouZou, 27

Note to Parents, Teachers, and Librarians
This Words I Know book uses full-color photographs and a nonfiction format to introduce the concept of language and parts of speech. *A Mouthful of Onomatopoeia* is designed to be read aloud to a pre-reader or to be read independently by an early reader. Photographs help listeners and early readers understand the text and concepts discussed. The book encourages further learning by including the following sections: Table of Contents, Read More, and Internet Sites. Early readers may need assistance using these features.

Printed in the United States 5798

Table of Contents

What's Onomatopoeia? 4
Animal Chatter 6
Water Fun 8
Get Moving 10
Open Wide 12
Two by Two 14
What Did You Say? 16
Surprise! 18
Near the Pond 20
Catch a Cold 22
Things That Go 24
Dig In! 26
Here, Birdie Birdie 28
Extra Fun 30

Read More 32
Internet Sites 32

What's Onomatopoeia?

Zip goes the jacket.
Grrr says the dog.

That was onomatopoeia (ah-nuh-mah-tuh-PEE-uh)!

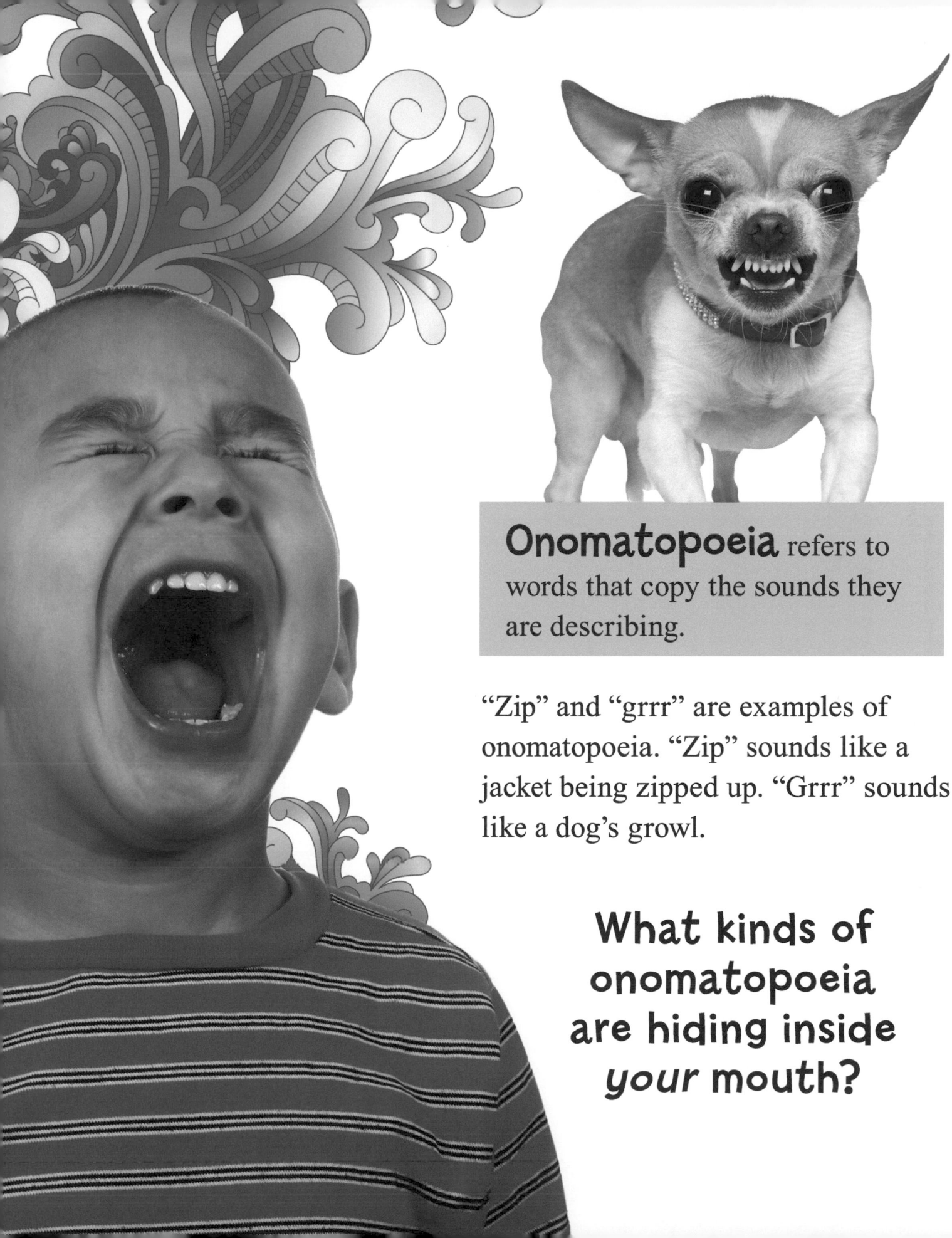

Onomatopoeia refers to words that copy the sounds they are describing.

"Zip" and "grrr" are examples of onomatopoeia. "Zip" sounds like a jacket being zipped up. "Grrr" sounds like a dog's growl.

What kinds of onomatopoeia are hiding inside *your* mouth?

Animal Chatter

What sound do ducks make? Donkeys? Dogs?
How about horses? Hippos? Hogs?

roar
woof
purr
howl

baa
arf
moo
growl

Water Fun

A waterpark is the place to be,
beating the heat and shouting, "WHEE!"

squish
slush
squirt
burble

glug
slap
plop
gurgle

drip
drizzle
swoosh
trickle
splash
spray
splatter
sprinkle

Get Moving

When something moves, listen up!
You might hear "BOING!" or "GLUP! GLUP! GLUP!"

plink
snip
clunk
smack
clank
bang
ring
thwack

Open Wide

This list of words says, "AHHH!" and shows the onomatopoeia in your mouth and nose.

smooch

shh

sniff

wah-wah

grunt

chuckle

yawn

ha-ha

ahem
hee-hee
whistle
hush
snore
yeow
stutter
shush

Two by Two

Sometimes words have more impact when they star as a double act.

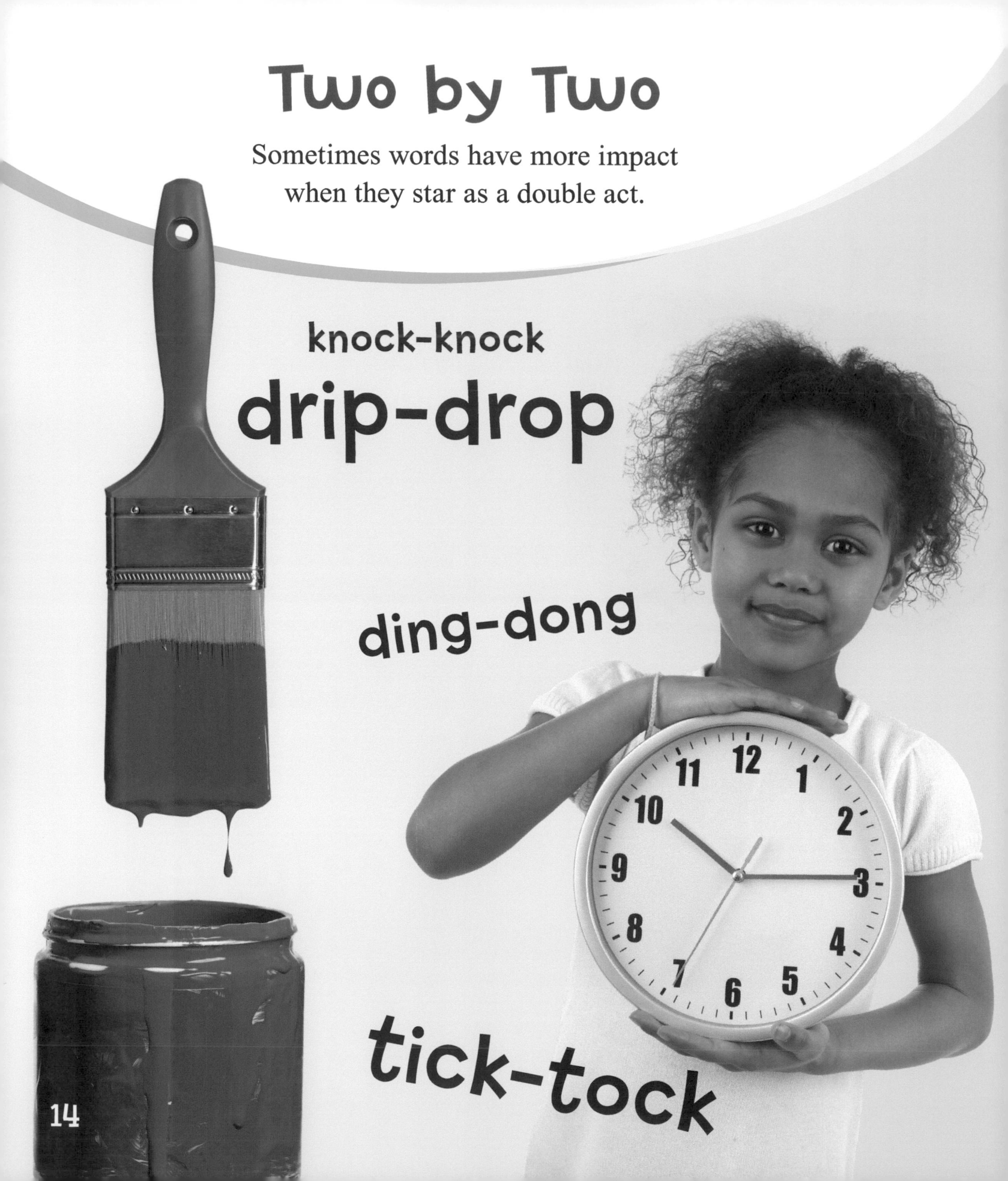

ping-pong
jingle-
jangle

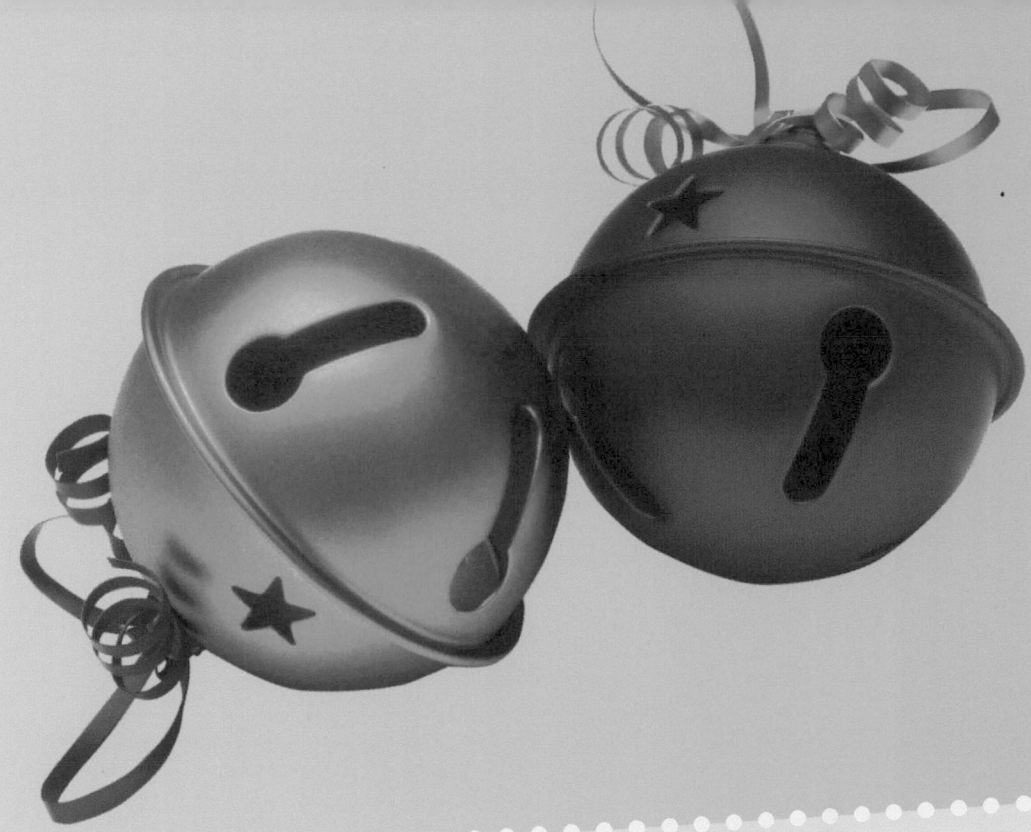

pitter-patter

flip-flop

What Did You Say?

So many ways to make yourself heard ...
Read through the list, then pick a word!

bawl
murmur
shriek
grumble

whoop
whine
blab
mumble

giggle
chatter
wail
whisper
snicker
blurt
mutter
whimper

Surprise!

Here's a surprise, just for you.
Will it make you jump or cry, "WHOO HOO"?

thud

tremble

boom

eek

Near the Pond

Critters that hop, crawl, and fly
make noise in the water and the weeds nearby.

rattle
croak
whirr
snap
ribbit
drone
flitter
splat

Catch a Cold

Grab a tissue, and get some rest.
Before too long, you'll be back to your best!

sniffle
barf
OW
groan
hack
ooze
gargle
moan

Things That Go

Cars and trucks and things that go ...
Are there words here you don't know?

rumble
screech
sputter
zoom
rev
shimmy
toot
vroom

Dig In!

Wash your hands. Take a seat.
Grab your fork. It's time to eat!

spit
belch
fizz
slurp

Here, Birdie Birdie

Some sing sweetly. Some sound strange.
Bird calls cover quite a range.

cackle
coo
twitter
peep

caw
tweet
trill
cheep

chirp
cluck
flutter
cuckoo
hoot
squawk
cock-a-doodle-doo

Extra Fun

Onomatopoeia is so much fun!
Want a little more before we're done?

yikes
bumble
crackle
sizzle

bleh
whack
wallop
fizzle

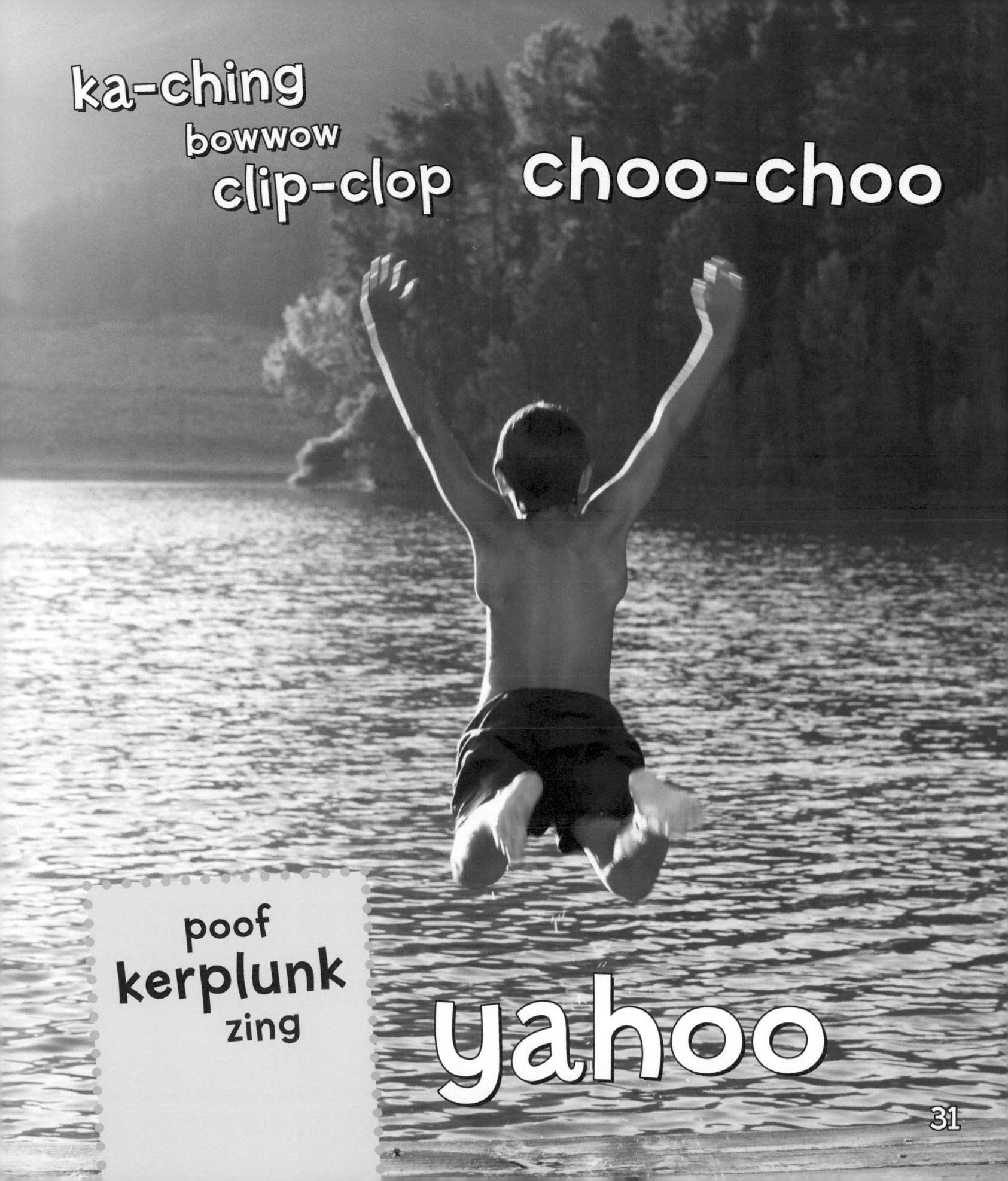
ka-ching
bowwow
clip-clop
choo-choo
poof
kerplunk
zing
yahoo

Read More

Aylesworth, Jim. *Cock-a-Doodle-Do, Creak, Pop-Pop, Moo.* New York: Holiday House, 2012.

DePalma, Mary Newell. *Bow, Wow Wiggle-Waggle.* Grand Rapids, Mich.: Eerdmans Books for Young Readers, 2012.

Marsalis, Wynton. *Squeak! Rumble! Whomp! Whomp! Whomp!: A Sonic Adventure.* Somerville, Mass.: Candlewick, 2012.

Internet Sites

FactHound offers a safe, fun way to find Internet sites related to this book. All of the sites on FactHound have been researched by our staff.

Here's all you do:

Visit *www.facthound.com*

Type in this code: 9781476539393